MI

For Jhon Bertha

Gosper.

MILES AWAY

JASPER MILES

Paper Doll

© Jasper Miles, 1998

First Published in 1998 by
Paper Doll
Belasis Hall,
Coxwold Way,
Billingham,
Cleveland.

All rights reserved.
Unauthorised duplication
contravenes existing laws.

ISBN : 1 86248 025 7

Typeset and Printed by
Lintons Printers, Co. Durham.

*To Jane, my wife,
for putting up with me when I write.*

*The poem 'Dancing' on page 11
previously published in
The Thetford and Breckland magazine.*

CONTENTS

Simple Poet	1
Moggies	2
Dogs	3
Horses	5
God's Sense Of Humour	7
Recognised	9
Christmas When Young	10
Dancing	11
Mr Average	13
The Wonderland	14
A Bowler Remembers	16
Her From Up The Road	17
Vandals	18
English Trouble	19
Tribute	20
Distant Poet (If Reincarnation Works?)	20
My Pet Hate	21
Christian Belief	23
Thoughts Of One Who Considered Holy Orders	24
The Woodlands	25
Little Brother Is Watching You	27
Lament Of A Lyric Poet	28
Law Of The Wild	29
Jennie Wren	31
Brock The Badger	31
Nature That I See	32
The Dividing Line	34
Poachers	35
If You Want To Know The Wood	37
Ornithological Query?	38

They Fulfil A Need	39
Gamekeepers	40
Keep Our Country, Country!	42
God's Gift	43
Soho	45
Charing Cross	45
Saint Bartholemew's	46
A Tree Of History	46
Agincourt	47
Lapdogs	49
Lock, Stock And Barrel	50
Flash In The Pan	51
Moonrakers	52
How Flavouring Commenced (A Fable)	54
Has Shot His Bolt?	55
King Charlie's Legacy	56
Ice-Houses	57
Three Times Whittington	58
Calling-Birds	59
A Sassenach's Lament For The Stuarts	61

SIMPLE POET

On this little world, 'round its little sun in a
                                    middling galaxy
Sits a little man with a little pen and great
                                          expectancy
Of converting some upon this world to think the
                                        same as he
By things he writes and themes he cites in simple
                                          poetry.
But other men can wield the pen with greater
                                          fluency
And their written word is often heard amongst the
                                      powers that be
But he'll still write, for he knows he's right; that
                                      simple poet: Me!

MOGGIES

I admit to liking doggies
Much more than moggies!
(Not wishing to offend
As there's been the feline friend)
My choice is Siamese
Failing that Burmese
Because oriental moggies
Behave more like doggies.

DOGS

I have always loved dogs and little puppy 'Sprog'
                                                  dogs!
Gun dogs, fun dogs, mucky dogs and lucky dogs
Scrounging dogs and lounging dogs,
Lazing by the fire dogs, drop-you-in-the-mire
                                                  dogs
Grotty dogs and spotty dogs, doubt regarding sire
                                                  dogs
Guard dogs, hard dogs, kennel-out-the-back dogs
Black dogs, track dogs, never win for me dogs
Hairy dogs and 'fairy' dogs, carried by their
                                         mistress dogs
Never let you in dogs, always make a din dogs,
Very, very fine dogs, 'All I do is whine' dogs,
'I can sit and beg' dogs, 'I lift up my leg' dogs
Always want a run dogs, nick a cake or bun dogs,
'Master? Let me come?' dogs, 'I will bite your
                                                 bum' dogs
Grinning as they greet dogs, 'Do I get a sweet?'
                                                 dogs
Sleigh dogs, stray dogs, always in the way dogs
Barge dogs, large dogs, very, very fat dogs
Yappy dogs and snappy dogs 'I'm scared of the
                                               cat' dogs
Smelly dogs, watch telly dogs, growl at
                                    Aussie-soap dogs
Sniffy dogs and whiffy dogs, 'Not a bath I hope?'
                                                dogs
Scruffy dogs and wuffy dogs, chew-up master's
                                            boot dogs

Muddy dogs and bloody dogs and couldn't care a hoot dogs
Hot dogs, sausage dogs, special breed by Heinz dogs
Sneaky dogs and leaky dogs, Beauty shop design dogs
Forgotten dogs and rotten dogs (Sorry! They are human dogs)
Think that they can talk dogs, run-off on their walk dogs
Pet dogs, wet dogs 'Take me to the vet' dogs
Hound dogs, found dogs, bark at any sound dogs
'Take me in the car' dogs, lead you to the bar dogs
More dogs and more dogs, more than I can tell dogs
And I must be a stupid hound? I still love ruddy dogs.

HORSES

A horse is an animal with four legs; one in each
                                                        corner,
A design feature adopted by many of the fauna,
And these legs each terminating in one hoof
Which was once toe or fingernail; no spoof!
These nails, having grown together provide those
                                              clippety clops
When the horse is in motion, but of course cease
                                              when it stops
Their sound is often accentuated as metal shoes
                                              are nailed
By farrier or plater, according to who was
                                                    detailed.

Your horse, now mobile, can be both groomed
                                                and fed
The feeding takes place at one end, where is
                                              placed its head;
This eats grass of its own volition, in stables
                                              usually hay,
Apples, carrots; sometimes a few oats and your
                                            peppermints by the way!
Grooming means brushing, cleaning and tending
                                            from tail to head;
The tail being at the far end, above waste-
                                        disposal: Nuff said!
Fit him (or her) with a saddle, bridle and etcetera
                                              called tack
And then, if it is in a good mood, climb, facing
                                            forward, onto its back.

Horses come in sizes and types, including ponies
                              which come smaller;
And these are measured by hands which indicate
                              tall or taller;
Steeple-chasers, hunters, brumbies in Australia,
                              mustangs in The States
Welsh and Shetland ponies and littler fellers seen
                              at shows and fêtes
There are also cavalry-horses, ridden by polished
                              soldiers on parade
And some, at equine rest-homes, no longer able
                              to make the grade.
Horse have cousins called donkeys and asses,
                              sometimes named mokes
The ass, crossed on her back, because of whom
                              she carried for us folks.

GOD'S SENSE OF HUMOUR

I'm sure that God has humour! It's as plain as the
                                   nose on your face
We need no tale or rumour leaked from the
                                   Throne of Grace,
Just look around creation and see his works
                                   displayed!
Give your consideration after this survey is made.

When slipping on your backside, think, who
                                   made the ice?
Who nettled and thistled the wayside? Who
                                   made fleas and lice?
Who taught the owl to 'oller when you're out on
                                   your own at night?
Made echo of footsteps follow? Made bowels go
                                   loose in fright.

Who made cows that packet in that bit of grass
                                   you tread?
Made morning-chorus racket when you plan to
                                   lay abed?
Surprises come to rock us, just when we're
                                   feeling fine?
Memories returning to mock us? Could that be
                                   humour divine?

Who fixes-up deflation when we're all puffed-up
                                   with pride?
Who ruins relaxation by giving us woman as
                                   bride?

Made a camel's hump and motion? Gave crests
                              to cockatoo?
And I'm sure there was humorous notion when
                        Almighty God made you.

RECOGNISED

I took my daughters to the zoo
As many parents often do
And there, within a cage of iron
Stood a proud and regal lion
Which turned its head and looked my way
And then behaved as if to say,
With attempts at lion smiles
'I recognise you! Jasper Miles?'

The passing crowd was quite forgot
As I stood rooted to the spot
Wondering, what did Leo feel?
Did he see me as a meal,
Raw or nicely boiled in stew?
Was I like someone he knew?
But something, deep within me, told
That he and I were friends of old.

He sadly watched me go my way,
I'm sure he wished that I would stay,
He did not want to see me leave
And I can very well believe
That something stirred inside his heart
Because we had once more to part.
On what ancient, distant shore
Could I have known that lion before?

CHRISTMAS WHEN YOUNG

Strips of coloured paper and a little bowl of paste
Making links of paper-chain in pre-war style and taste
Along with bits of evergreen upon the window sill
At our village infant class; the season of goodwill.

In one hallowed corner stands the stable scene
The baby in the manger, the virgin clothed in green,
Joseph and the shepherds and a slightly damaged king;
A page cut from a carol book says 'Hark! The
                                    angels sing'.

And there are rows of drawings stuck upon the wall,
Most of us drew angels with wings and harps and all
Much artistic licence has to be allowed;
Some look more like vultures in that 'heavenly' crowd.

Then there is our Christmas tree, just inside the door
Dropping lots of needles down upon the floor,
With tinsel, bells and packages, cotton-wool for snow
And on the top a fairy with tinted cheeks aglow.

And we are learning carols to sing for mums and dads
Along with older classes and the local choir lads
And then we have our holidays for Christmas and
                                    New Year;
I hope that Santa won't forget. 'Please Santa? Be a
                                    dear!'

DANCING

I wish that I'd learnt to dance
Missing out on many a chance
Of enjoying the charms
Of a girl in my arms
How I wish that I'd learnt to dance.

I Waltzed like a left-footed horse
Making other mistakes of course
And I near made a gaff
With a big-busted Waaf
Fixing grounds for divorce.

My Quick-Step was never quite right
I'm told an unusual sight
With a Land-Girl in breeches,
My mates were in stitches,
It seemed alright; I was tight!

My Fox-Trot's a riot I'm told
Once tried in the rural wold
At a public house
With the landlord's spouse
And my! But that hussy was bold.

My Tango is something to see
But somehow a nurse and me
Won a prize on the floor
How? I'm not sure!
Inebriated? Maybe?

At hops in the Sergeants' Mess
I really must confess
Of some partners I'd wonder
Just what they had under
That flowing evening dress.

Yes I wish that I'd learned to dance,
Looking back as the years advance,
But at least you will know
I was no gigolo:
But is it too late to chance?

MR AVERAGE

I suppose, some ways, I am an average bloke
The suits I wear are not bespoke
No fortune in the bank, but not quite broke
The horse I back performs like Riley's moke

Old What's-It? Luck is always on his side
Since he was his mummy's pride
A lovely job and home, and lovely bride
Life all down-hill; a pleasant, gentle glide.

But is he really better off, I ask
With time and wherewithal to bask
Whilst I go forth to do my task
Putting on a doubtful, cheerful mask?

But I am knowing more than What's-It knows
Like how to rise when falling on my nose,
Standing firm no matter how luck flows
And fight against the bitter wind that blows

Life, in my belief, is made so we can learn
With wisdom as the wages one can earn.
Though living What's-It's way I sometimes yearn;
I have some wisdom: never his concern.

THE WONDERLAND

What are you seeking Grandpa, your eyes set on
                                       the sky?
You do not seem to notice us, nor hear our
                                       playful cries
What is it that you're seeing? Is there something
                                       really there?
Tell us please oh Grandpa? We see nothing
                                       though we stare.

Up there is the Welkin, the place of clouds, its
                                       name,
'Tis where I often travelled long years before you
                                       came
For when I was a young man, I flew up there
                                       above
And I was paid to do so; my work I used to love.

My mates and I loved flying, both in war and
                                       peace
The Air, our Mistress, bonded us; she never
                                       gives release!
Most of us would fly again throughout our
                                       closing years,
Up above is Magic which can even now bring
                                       tears.

We've seen the land below us like a spread out
                                       patchwork quilt
We have flown above great deserts where towns
                                       are seldom built,

Our wings have crossed the oceans, passed jungle, hill and plain,
Arctic, temperate, tropic, and we'd do it all again.

And up there is Wonderland; I've seen it once or twice
Approached at night through heavy cloud which isn't always nice
With turbulence in blackness, with but instruments to guide
To then burst forth in moonlight, like in wondrous fairy ride

Ones plane is turned to silver as the towering castles pass
Aerials turned to tinsel, the perspex? Crystal glass,
You fly through snow-filled valleys beneath the moon so bright
The clouds are glorious mountains, all bathed in mystic light.

And then you find a snow-field leading endlessly to space
Over which you're skimming at exhilarating pace,
Formating on your shadow as it follows just below;
One lovely sight of nature just for flying boys to know.

So when your Grandpa's sitting with eyes set on the skies
See you don't disturb him with games and playful cries
And if he does not hear you, just try to understand
That Grandpa could be flying in his magic wonderland.

A BOWLER REMEMBERS

Had I a young man's legs
Along with a young man's arm
Whilst three bailled pegs
Stood waiting me to harm?
Complete would be my dream
With a one-side polished ball
And fingers down the seam
To swing and shatter all.

To once more beat the bat
By landing right on length:
I often managed that
In days of youth and strength.
Days! Oh days long past?
When I in red-marked whites,
Though never really fast
Could give good batsmen frights.

HER FROM UP THE ROAD

I could have sworn it was her, from up the road,
Carrying a pathetic little load
Among the refugees of somewhere like Bosnia,
Or was it Kurdistan? Serbia? Croatia?
Refugees are all alike, the same people walking
Going somewhere better, seldom talking
Save occasionally for the newsreel
Too embittered to say what they really feel
But the very same folk, the very same faces
That we saw in other years and other places
One looking like her from up the road
Kid on her arm and a shouldered load.
I wonder! Will ever she watch TV
And see a stumbling old refugee? Me?

VANDALS

Vandals, in the history book that I read as a boy,
Had doctrine of our modern ones, Destroy!
                              Destroy! Destroy!
But Vandals seldom see the truth regarding what
                                       they do
They are destroying their own needs as well for
                                       me and you.
Let us take phone-boxes, they oft put out of use.
For death can be resultant because of this abuse
As, after they have 'fixed' a box, a fire or accident
Has urgency of nine-nine-nine but time must thus
                                       be spent
Searching for another phone and meanwhile
                                       someone dies;
It happens! Yes! It happens! So don't look with
                                       surprise!
I pose them this scenario. You've just done the
                                       deed
And stepped into a passing car? Whose is now the
                                       need?
Should some compassionate person run to make a
                                       call?
Or leave you lying, dying? Think it through.
                                       That's all.

ENGLISH TROUBLE

The Scotsman and the Welshman criticise the
                                               English
With nationalist aversion regarding staying
                                               British
But I ask the question:- What English do they
                                               mean?
And I ask it as an Englishman whose ancestry is
                                               clean.

Nearly every Englishman has forebears who were
                                               Scottish,
Others have Welsh grandmas and uncles who are
                                               Irish
Thus English who are Englishmen are thin upon
                                               the ground
Just hear an 'English' council and listen to the
                                               sound.

'Ye canna get awa' wi' that' cries a voice from
                                               o'er the Border
'Listen! Look-you boyyo! You are once more
                                               out of order.'
The same is true of Parliament, few English,
                                               mostly crossbred!
And I know I'll be in trouble because this truth
                                               I've said.

TRIBUTE

'If' can be a stupid word when dealing with the
                                                  past
For what is done, is ever done, it's history to last.
If only this? If only that? Won't change a thing
                                                  one jot
Whatever happened, happened and you've got just
                                          what you've got.

But 'If' can be a real help concerning future tense
For 'If' can help decisions in time that's coming
                                                  hence
The greatest 'If' to help a man, is, in my humble
                                              thinking,
'If' by the Master-Poet, my mentor, Rudyard
                                              Kipling.

DISTANT POET
(IF REINCARNATION WORKS?)

Is there in my karmic history, a poet, Me?
And I wonder in what age that it could be?
And wonder too if traits come through from he?
And did he write the works he liked and free,
Or were his words for master's flattery
To gain him fame and a life of luxury?
Do I ever read the works of me when he?

MY PET HATE

Oh why did Mr Logie Baird experiment with
                                      vision?
I've seen the 'box' near fifty years and view it
                                      with derision,
I don't agree with half I see and some I even hate
Infernal, childish, ruddy 'Soaps'! Oh when will
                                      they abate?
Why not one single channel for those who like
                                      such trash
With all the con-trick adverts for folk to waste
                                      their cash?

Those ghastly cooking programmes put me in a
                                      bilious state
They've turned me off most dishes that I used to
                                      think were great
With herbs I think are horrid and loads of olive
                                      oil
And then of course the garlic! (This sets my
                                      blood aboil)
I'm Brit not ruddy Gascon! Not Itie nor a Greek
Let that lot stink of garlic! I can't stand that
                                      awful reek!

The 'News' and allied programs? I watch with
                                      jaundiced eye!
Stories bent and laundered, just short of barefaced
                                      lie
But information slanted for to give the wrong
                                      impressions

(The venomous denials seem like tender-spot
                                confessions):
I was around in war-time; heard Haw-Haw's
                                  nightly tale:
I feel what we're getting now would turn old
                                  Goebbels pale.

Oh blasted television? You would try to run our
                                  lives
Remember sex, for some of us, is private, with
                                  our wives
And seeing couples 'at it' when we switch a
                                  programme on
Is not average parent's choice for daughter or
                                  their son.
I say to programme masters who choose the
                                  things we view,
Stop trying to control our minds, or we'll end up
                                  low as you.

CHRISTIAN BELIEF?

I'm told by Christian teachers, we may not whip
                                            nor kill
Criminals who murder and practice crimes of ill
They say we follow Jesus who whipped the
                                         Temple 'thieves'
And God, who slays for lying, or so 'The Acts'
                                               believes?

Others more committed, would have me keep off
                                                  meat
But Jesus at 'The Supper' had his lamb to eat?
And then there was Elijah! And, in case you
                                         never heard?
God, seeing he was hungry, sent flesh by raven
                                                bird?

Only fools like warfare but at times we have to
                                                fight
But certain 'Peaceful Christians' deny we have
                                             that right
And to impede us doing so, they sit-down in the
                                                way
Oh will they hold a protest on Armaggedon's day?

THOUGHTS OF ONE WHO
CONSIDERED HOLY ORDERS

My plan of life was the regular service, all the lot
Then, taking Holy Orders, become some parish Sky-Pilot.
Of course I married, left the mob and became a rep:
Ruining my plan but I never really regretted that step.
For priesthood has changed so very much since I
                                            was a lad
And being regarded as many of the present would
                                            make me sad.
But, just think, if I had continued, and now
                          thundered from your pulpit?
If Hell was where you headed, you would have
                                  pre-knowledge of it.

Most may think this a figment of my poetic imagination?
But no! Truthfully! It was thusward I thought my
                                            destination
And I realised, as such, knowledge of my subject
                                      would be the need
And I read the necessary books which should
                                    ensure I would succeed;
Things the Church opposed, I investigated to be
                                      sure of my ground
Hence, now I am a psychic and consider such
                                      practices are sound.
Then let's consider sin? And I ask, with a knowing grin,
Could I, as priest, guide thee away from paths I'd never
                                                bin?

THE WOODLANDS

I've read about the woodlands by those who view
                                        the scene
And speak of perfect paradise within its leafy
                                        green;
Idyllic little pictures - the mother deer with fawn,
A songbird's nest with spotted eggs, cubs at play
                                        at dawn.

That knee-deep pile of bluebells as they carpet
                                        'neath the trees
And pretty wild anemones, head nodding in the
                                        breeze,
That hidden clump of primroses growing in the
                                        dell
But who writes of the woodland that's more akin
                                        to Hell?

The talon rules the woodland, with beak and
                                        tooth and claw
All weapons of destruction which work God's
                                        natural law.
Your darling fawn will grow a buck and in this
                                        regal state
At time of rut, fight bloody war, for privilege to
                                        mate.

That clutch of eggs will never hatch but make a
                                        jay-bird's meal
For nature has its burglars that live by what they
                                        steal,

Each furry cub becomes a fox, as such will kill for fun
And slaughter fifty pullets once in your chicken run.

Reynard when kill-crazy leaves not a pretty sight
He'll clear a sea-bird colony just visiting one night.
(Some will call me anti-fox and argue black is blue,
Me? I speak from knowledge and know my words are
                                                                      true.)

Then look below your bluebells among the fallen leaf
Here's a world of bloodshed and pain beyond belief.
Bird, animal or insect, each needs its belly filled
And all are subject to the law 'Kill or you'll be
                                                                   killed'.

Go! Seek in any woodland, and this time really look!
You'll find in one half-acre all crime that's in the book.
Yet still I love the woodland, despite of what I know
Of murder foul there taking place, inches from my toe.

Bred, born and raised as 'keeper, to listen, see and
                                                                   care,
My love of English woodland is a very old affair,
And that is an enigma as no doubt this verse will tell;
But don't write woodland stories 'less it's the truth as
                                                                   well.

LITTLE BROTHER IS WATCHING YOU

You? Under constant surveillance! Thus be well
                                                 aware!
Your actions monitored and noted as you enter
                                                 there
Viewed from all angles, left, right, centre, above
                                          and below
Eyes following your every movement wherever
                                                you go.
Your intentions are deliberated upon; are they
                                          evil or good?
The conclusions being vital to those denizens of
                                          the wood.

Tiny little creatures observe your every act
You are their worst enemy; that's a simple fact
And if you really listen you will hear the
                                         songbirds call;
Not his usual trilling but a red alert to all
For every bird and animal that is feeling, hearing
                                                seeing
Lives its life in constant fear of you, oh human
                                                being.

LAMENT OF A LYRIC POET

Blank verse is a curse m'dear
Beloved of publishers I fear
Invented for those who cannot rhyme
Or lazy ones who don't have time
To find the words for lyric English
And use intellectual gibberish
Encouraging a self-important band
Who claim to understand
The message of the writer's intent
Wondering why so little is spent
By average folks on poetry books:
Mention you're a poet and see the looks?

LAW OF THE WILD

Make a mistake in everyday life and most times
                                you'll get through
But to make a mistake in the natural world can
                                mean the end of you
Place your foot on a busy road and the
                                approaching car will hoot
But place your foot on a deadly snake? Just hope
                                it strikes your boot.
Put your hand in an open till and you well may
                                get probation
But put your hand on a lion's cub and your bits
                                are for cremation.

Drugs can give euphoric state, leaving
                                depressions to follow
Some plants in the wild may taste quite mild but
                                they are death to swallow
Mother nature has no care of the laws we humans
                                make
Her law is 'Always be aware in every step you
                                take'
You well may wander in your mind at the side of
                                a London street
But out in the wild you learn as a child you are
                                only so much meat.

Now you may think in this pleasant land that
                                Nature's law is out
But you should care and be aware in life as you
                                go about

We still have adders on the heath, and poisonous plants still grow,
And a cow with a calf still sometimes acts like a raging buffalo
You're responsible for your life, thus you must be aware!
And a caring social worker won't help one bit out there.

JENNIE WREN

There used to be a day (I've lost its name)
When villagers set out upon a very serious game,
In hunting, finding and killing little Jennie Wren
For it was the Devil's bird, or so they thought it
                                                              then;
Later priests would bless them for (Nutty though
                                                             it sounds)
Driving Mr Satan from their parish bounds.

BROCK THE BADGER

Dried cow-pats overturned?
Now! By the lore I've learned!
Brother Brock? Twas done by thee!
Thy snout turned them, for to see,
A gourmet snack to be,
The bugs and beetles running free
All meet for thy cavernous throat
Thou? Omnivorous as any goat,
Save brother goat does not kill
And I know well you will.

NATURE THAT I SEE

I will speak about the nature that I see
In every wayside hedge and every tree.
Like the fragile turtle-dove
Which purrs its song of love;
There's always bits of nature there for me.

Sometimes in the nature there for me
The frightened little songbirds scream a plea
When a hovering kestrel swoops
Or the speedy falcon stoops
For nature's not all pretty that I see.

There are certain hidden flowers that I see
On the bank along the rill and in the lea,
There are places that I know
Where the wild orchids grow;
Such things I keep as secret that I see.

It is best to keep as secret what I see!
If I tell? Then others follow me;
They release their yapping pets
Even play their radio sets!
And make barren where those flowers ought to be.

Thus I never tell of otters that I see
Or location of their holt that's known to me;
If I do? Then this my reason,
Naught will be there that next season
And no more otters ever there to see.

If you really love the country? Be like me
And never tell about the things you see
For if you go and say
Then hordes will pass that way
And what they go to see will go and flee.

The weasel, stoat and fox I often see;
They are vermin in the country I agree
But the vermin I would ban
Is the thoughtless breed of man,
As, long ago my father said to me.

THE DIVIDING LINE

Observing in the countryside the creatures small
                                  and great,
I'm often led to wonder as regards their mental state;
What do they do by instinct? What by intelligence?
What is programmed in them? What's done by
                                commonsense?
'Twixt thought and auto-actions! Where do we
                                draw the line?
Smarter brains than I possess, cannot that line define.

Consider higher animals which have more
                                complex minds.
They say the chimpanzee is top in out of water kinds?
And from monkey ancestry mankind is said to come;
Evolution changes causing what we have become
But where in mental progress came right or
                                wrong as choice
And individual effort, not just by instinct's voice?

Where in this evolution (If that's the way we came?)
Did we act independently instead of all the same?
When did minds start worrying about the good
                                and bad?
Whence came that past decisions could make men
                                sad or glad?
When too did troubled conscience start mankind
                                acting odd?
Evolutionary progress? I trace the hand of God.

POACHERS

When I was just a lad and walking with my dad, I
    saw a piece of china in the grass.

My father saw as well, saying 'Listen to me well!
    Someone's set a snare near where we pass.'

So we took a look around and a well-set snare we
    found; said dad 'Old Ted is poaching once
        again.'

With little need for talk we continued on our
    walk, the broken bits of china showing plain

Each led us to a snare and you may not think this
    fair but we moved the china markers on our route

But every poaching man must expect his well laid
    plan ruined by the keeper of the shoot.

One old keeper that I knew, and I've knowledge
    of a few, painted fox-repellent on some snares,

(You very well may think that you know a rotten
    stink? But get a whiff of this stuff unawares!)

The result was empty snares for no rabbits and no
    hares had audacity or stomach to come near

And other ways dad taught, can turn snaring's
    worth to nought, but me tell you? The answer is
        'No Fear!'

There is one thing I'll tell, and mark it very well!
    Your average poacher is a common thief.

Your romantic novels paint some slightly
    tarnished saint; a Robin Hood who roves the
        woods with stealth

But he does not take a pheasant for some local,
hungry peasant, he takes it for himself or his own
        wealth.

And game's not all he'll take for he's always 'On
    the make', lifting anything that's left around

So listen what I'm telling, leave nothing fit for
selling, if a man who's known for poaching walks
        your ground.

IF YOU WANT TO KNOW THE WOOD

If you want to know the wood?
Then learn it as you should
And keep your wits about you as you walk.
Open up your ear and eye
To notice what's nearby
From creepy-crawlies to the speeding hawk.

There's the pheasant who goes 'Cock!'
And the badger we call 'brock'
And often there's a squirrel in a tree;
Make looking-out your habit
Then you'll spot each bunny-rabbit
And every stoat and weasel running free.

See each pigeon flying by,
Note that kestrel in the sky
And every little songbird on the wing;
Each has its separate call,
Get to know them one and all:
They make a lovely chorus when they sing.

Learn to walk with silent tread,
Keep your tongue within your head
And do your woodland-watching without sound
Try standing very still
You'll see more if you will
And thus you know more wild-life that's around.

It's the way that I was taught
When I was three-foot-nought
A lesson that I learnt, and learnt it good!
For my father taught me well
And this is why I tell
To look and listen silent in the wood.

ORNITHOLOGICAL QUERY?

The heron was prey to the falconer's bird
Which would climb to approach in a dive I've heard,
And the stork-like victim went on its back
Attempting impaling the hawk in attack.

I have watched birds since when a child
But never seen falcons in the wild
Attack the herons lumbering by
There must be a reason. I'm asking why?

THEY FULFIL A NEED

Have you ever noticed the job of weeds?
For the gardener? The last of his needs,
For they will grow whatever he should sow
And their appearance seldom slow.
But, if you look where land is ripped bare?
Weeds, like a plaster-dressing appear
As though to cover the open sore
With vegetation on the surface once more.

GAMEKEEPERS

They conserved the country ere we heard of
                              conservation,
They kept clear the woodland and saw to
                              preservation,
Kept predatory carnivores numerically
                              manageable,
Through them we have a rural scene both pretty
                              and agreeable;
Of course they reared the partridge and they
                              reared the pheasant
But consider, if without them, we would have a
                              land so pleasant?

Wander in the country where there's been no
                              keeper's hand
And you notice dereliction taking o'er the land;
You say that you love songbirds? Do you notice
                              they are rare?
Do you ever wonder why so very few are there?
Then notice jays and magpies in profusion all
                              around?
'Tis they that rob the nests of eggs in tree or on
                              the ground.

Some will tell that nature has the balance well in
                              hand
At least so say the know-it-alls but do they
                              understand?
What jay or magpie predator keeps those two in
                              check?

Just your local keeper and he gets it in the neck
If they should see him shoot one or arranging
                                they get caught:
Do-gooders of the countryside, cry he didn't
                                ought.

Who kept down the weasels? Who kept down the
                                stoats?
Who kept down the rabbits that ate the wheat and
                                oats?
Before the Myxomatosis (The rabbit's beaten
                                that)
Of course the keeper took the 'can' for everyone's
                                lost cat
But if old keepers were so bad as now do-gooders
                                rate
How came anything survived their dozens each
                                estate?

Born to be a keeper, I know the truth I speak
Of men who never rested seven days a week;
True old keepers loved their work; you just ask
                                their wives!
Their birds, their woods and wild-life! Sum total
                                of their lives.
Because of them this Britain has a decent
                                countryside
And my gamekeeper ancestry is this old Briton's
                                pride.

KEEP OUR COUNTRY, COUNTRY!

If you come to the country and you sit down to eat
Don't leave your picnic wrappers like rubbish in the street
We cannot have grass-sweepers like those that clean your roads
For living there are animals like voles and mice and toads.

If you come in the country and you stop to have a drink
Don't drop your empty bottles, for if you stop and think,
You know that broken glass is sharp; you do not need the proof.
Then imagine painful damage it can do a horse's hoof?

If you come to the country, then learn to close the gates
As cattle grazing in his crops is what a farmer hates
For gates are there to regulate what can or not pass through
And if you leave them open then the farmer will stop you.

We live in the country and we do not like the mess
Left by unthinking 'Townies' to cause our beasts distress
We know you don't like living in a dirty, mucky road,
Remember in the country, there is a Country Code.

GOD'S GIFT

Adam roved the countryside and he was feeling
                                                                                     low
Remembering Eden's garden when he lived there
                                                                                  long ago
Wishing he had never sinned and was welcome
                                                                 once again
And still he mourned for Abel, killed by his
                                                           brother Cain;
Eve, of course, had borne him Seth but emptiness
                                                              remained
'Oh God? I'm feeling lonely!' he silently
                                                              complained.

He wandered on then found a seat upon a fallen
                                                                    log
But there he heard the whimper of a tiny
                                                          wolf-cub dog,
No sign of the mother wolf, nor pack that he
                                                            could see;
He picked the little fellow up and set it on his
                                                                knee.
At first, in fright, it tried to bite but soon it lost
                                                             the fear,
Then licked a hand as if to say 'I'm quite happy
                                                               here!'

When Adam later set off home, the puppy ran
                                                              behind
Thus it was a bond was forged 'twixt man and
                                                           canine kind;

The puppy grew, got civilised in dog and master
                                               state
Save once running to the woods, returning with a
                                                mate.
Puppies came, grew faithful, thus was the
                              friendship sealed.
Did God hear lonely Adam? That pup! His love
                                         revealed?

SOHO

Here, ere London burst its wall
There echoed 'Soho' hunting call,
The cry to tell the hare was sighted
Given where you are delighted
With grand cuisine, in restaurant hugged
And now the hare comes nicely jugged.

CHARING CROSS

The Royal Mews stood on this spot
Whence carriages at the trot
Came forth to carry Prince or King
Oft-times to the fanfare's ring
But ere the horses in this place
Lived hawks and falcons for the chase.

SAINT BARTHOLOMEW'S

'Tis said the King's Jester's wit
Hurt, as many would admit
And some, fearing Rahere at Court
Enquired if it could be bought?
The answer to this is not known
But neither did he ever own
How came the wherewithal
He founded both church and hospital?

A TREE OF HISTORY

Wherever we go there is something to know!
Say where the yew-trees grow?
For many, many years ago
From them we made our famed longbow.

That bow won Crecy and Poiters
And bloody Agincourt affair;
France's chivalry learnt to beware
When English archery crossed La Mare.

AGINCOURT

I never want to see a battle
Nor hear its fearful lethal rattle
But if from out of history's yield
I had to view one bloody field
Then I'd pick Agincourt.

I read how Harry's happy band,
No doubt through living off the land,
Had found their tummies rather free
For they were touched by dysentery
And often taken short.

The clothing then was woven thick
And not designed to come off quick,
Disrobing called for fingers slick
As buttons were a modern trick
And zips had not been thought.

'Tis said, as was the custom then,
These earthy English fighting men
Removed their tied-on pants from harm
And carried them upon their arm
Or something of the sort.

I saw Olivier on the screen
Show it as it might have been
But oh that he had set the scene
And showed the sight as really seen
'Twould ended up in court.

The ranks of archers, buttock bare,
Breeze be-ruffled pubic hair
To emphasise their manhood fair
Small wonder Frenchmen did despair
And tremble at the thought.

I bear an ancient English name
And thrill to Albion's fighting fame
But never did our yeomen rude
Excel the men who stood half-nude
To win the day at Agincourt.

LAP DOGS

Human beings young and old have aversion to
    the cold and often in the winter in my car

Those in the rear seat, cry 'Please turn up the
    heat!' before I've chance to travel very far.

Now think of coaching days? Ladies travelling
    on their ways, often found themselves a trifle
    chilly.

There was no electric heat to warm them in their
    seat and use of naked fire was rather silly.

Of course they often tried hot bottles on the ride
    but these were apt to lose their temperature.

Thus ladies wore warm clothes, woolly drawers I
    do suppose? And put their hands within big
    muffs of fur.

But the fur already hot was there for those who'd
    got a live and cuddly dog upon their lap.

The 'Lapdog' was the rage and we find on
    history's page, ladies spoilt to death the little
    chap.

And so, that scruffy tyke? Which doubtlessly you
    like, had ancestors they bred for ladies' laps.

Don't you love it when he licks? But excuse his
dirty tricks, like chewing gloves, and letting
                                    manners lapse.

LOCK, STOCK AND BARREL

'Lock, stock and barrel' a common cliché
If wanting the lot as well you may
Thus its meaning? Everything there!
Each cupboard, table and easy chair.

It seems to mean the lock on the door,
Stock in the shop on shelves and floor
And the barrels awaiting in the store
So nought or nothing is left anymore.

It did not mean that at the start,
In jargon of the gun-smith's art
Parts of every gun that's made
By skilled artificers in that trade.

Triggers fire by working the 'Lock',
The butt at your shoulder is the 'Stock'
The 'Barrel' spits the bullet or ball;
'Lock, Stock and Barrel' that is all.

FLASH IN THE PAN

You have heard people say 'A flash in the pan'
But do you know how this term began?
The pan is not of the frying brand
Nor salt-pan found in the desert sand
But on old muskets and blunderbusses
A flash in the pan could bring forth cusses
An intricate portion of the flintlock
With cover raised by the hammer cock
And explosive powder to be lit by the spark
Igniting and causing the gun to bark
For from the pan ran a little hole
To the powder charge in the barrel's bowl
And the flash of the powder in the pan,
Straight through to the charge it usually ran
But sometimes only the flash would appear
The gun did not fire; 'twas the soldier's fear.
And still one-offs who flash, then fail
Are a 'flash in the pan': so ends my tale.

THE FIRST MOONRAKERS

My father was a Wiltshireman, a Moonraker was he
And how they came to get that name he often told to me
When I was but a little lad I learnt the tale so well;
It is traditional history, this story that I tell.

There has been smuggling in the land since long, long, long ago
Of brandy and of 'baccy', not evil drugs we know!
Gaugers sought the smugglers to stop unlawful trade:
Some smugglers told this story of a crafty trick they played.

These smugglers had small barrels slung on their ponies' backs
But they knew the gaugers were following in their tracks
Then as they passed a wayside pond, reflection of the moon
Had their leader saying 'We play the country loon!'

The gaugers found some yokels, grouped at the waterside
And stopped to take a breather for long had been their ride,
The drunken yokels raking, and as nicely as you please,
Said that they were raking for 'That girt big shining cheese'

The laughing gaugers left them and got back on
                                          the trail.
Those yokels were the smugglers; so goes this
                                          rural tale
The rakes had held their barrels down and safely
                                          out of sight;
And Wiltshiremen are Moonrakers, since that
                                          moonlit night.

HOW FLAVOURING COMMENCED
(A FABLE)

Morg, advanced for his time, often asked when?
                             Where? And why?
'Why the moon and sun?' 'Why earth, sea and
                                      sky?'
Learnt of things around him and wishing more to
                                      know;
Whilst his tribe scattered seed, Morg sowed a row.
Crushing a leaf one day, a tantalizing smell he smelt
Making him conscious of how hungry he felt;
Hurrying off home, with appetite sharp and vast
From the cave-mouth fire, he drew forth a bear-meat
                                      repast
Which was tough, stringy, rank and very plain,
Deadening his palate, he returned it to cook again.
Disgruntled, Morg ruminated on the leaf which had
                       made his taste buds rise
Found the shrub and picked its leaves for
                             experimental enterprise.
Returning, he checked the haunch roasting in hot
                                      ash
Then, with stones, he smote his leaves into a pulpy
                                      mash
Which he larded onto the sizzling joint of meat;
Allowed it time to bubble, then cooled it to eat.
Later on he called the headmen who approved the
                                    meat so scented
Thus, in a short time, Morg's herb-garden got
                                      invented.

HAS SHOT HIS BOLT?

Now powerful was the crossbow
Its bolt, which was its arrow
Penetrated armour so they tell
But it needed aiming well
As reloading was not quick
And you could feel very sick
To shoot your bolt and fail
And find that man in mail,
One of the knighthood bold
Had you at his mercy, cold.
Thus 'Shoot your bolt' in any way
And probably you'll lose the day.
'Shot his bolt' has stuck around
Since war forgot the bowstring sound.

KING CHARLIE'S LEGACY

Have you thought who started this scientific age?
Or how he got it going, and on which historic
                              page?
Now I believe the culprit was our Merry
                         Monarch, Charlie
And it's dated from the moment when he formed
                         the Royal Society.
Up till then experimenters mostly worked alone
Thought crazy, or as witches; some, others would
                               not own!
But Charlie, he was one himself, worked on the
                         hand-grenade,
Called them all together to talk and secrets trade;
They, learning from each other, became a
                         knowledge bank
Then later on came Newton, so 'tis Charlie we
                            should thank.

ICE-HOUSES

Old mansions have a building which is oft
                              beneath a mound
As temperature required within is better under
                                     ground
Usually located on or near the lakeside shore;
They used it as an 'ice-house' though seldom any
                                         more.

In days before refrigerators these were piled with
                                            ice
Gathered in the winter for when days get hot and
                                            nice
And ice-cream was invented back in Charles the
                                  Second's reign
For this and cooling many things, ice-houses
                                    were a gain.

Sometimes there were passages running 'neath
                                    the ground
Connected to the kitchens: there's one I know
                                      around.
Our ancestors were seldom slow in creature
                                    comfort way
And you will find ice-houses still abound today.

THREE TIMES WHITTINGTON!

You've heard about Dick Whittington, Lord
                        Mayor of London thrice?
But Dick was three times buried, and that was not
                                      so nice,
They walled him in within his church and left
                                him there to rest
But twice they opened up the grave; 'tis truth and
                                    not a jest!

Rich as well as famous and the story soon got spread
Of treasure placed within the tomb where Dick
                                was lying dead.
The priest, who heard the rumour of wealth inside
                                the grave
Decided exhumation: an avaricious knave.

Thus he got some workmen but discovered
                                nothing there
He had them mend the damage which they did
                                with little care
And then the congregation grew painfully aware
That the odour of Dick's body was floating in the air.

They opened up the grave again or so 'Stowes
                                Survey' said.
This time they sealed Dick's body by lapping it in lead.
'Twas thus a most unworthy priest revealed his greedy
                                    vice
And Dick, three times as Lord Mayor, was also buried
                                      thrice.

CALLING-BIRDS

In days now gone, when catching duck, men used the 'duck-decoy'
As duck, forever curious; their weakness to employ,
And so upon the lakeside, a dog for duck to see
Usually a terrier sort, light-coloured, running free
In and out of hurdle-fence to catch the birds' attention
The curious duck then followed, which was the planned intention.

Those woven hurdles either side of water channel cut;
The dog appeared and disappeared, the way the hurdles put
The channel led beneath a net, formed to make a tunnel
A man behind, the duck flew in to find the net a funnel
Thus all the curious duck were caught within that duck-decoy
But then to get more duck to land, there was another ploy.

Tame duck swam that water to entice the migrant
                                               bird
'Call-duck' or the 'Calling-Birds' about the which
                                        you've heard?
Four are in the Christmas song, next to 'Three
                                        French Hens'
(I've seen them named as 'Collie Birds' by certain
                                     wayward pens!)
Ignoring dogs, these well-fed duck were oft with
                                     pinioned wing:
So now you'll know about them when 'tis
                         Christmas songs you sing.

A SASSENACH'S LAMENT FOR
THE STUARTS

On which side at Culloden were Scots in more
                                              profusion?
The answer to this question can cause a slight confusion.
It goes against those set ideas which are around today;
More fought for King Geordie, no matter what they say.

There were also English, fighting for the Bonnie Prince
(I realise there are readers who I never will convince)
But had I been around, and fit, I say without a pause;
No way am I papist but I'd hold the Stuart cause.

But there's the rub, religion, a bigot and a fool,
The Young Pretender's grandpa you read about in school
'Twas he that caused the trouble, and then he ran away
It's probable the seal he dropped is in the Thames today.

What! Oh what a pity! He was not more like his
                                                brother
Charles our Merry Monach; shall we never have
                                                another?
Oh had Bonnie Charlie won and sired a male offspring
To be like his great-uncle, Charles our brilliant King.